Deep, Deep Down

The Secret Underwater Poetry of the Mariana Trench

by Lydia Lukidis

illustrated by Juan Calle

CAPSTONE EDITIONS
a capstone imprint

Published by Capstone Editions, an imprint of Capstone.
1710 Roe Crest Drive, North Mankato, Minnesota 56003
capstonepub.com

Library of Congress Cataloging-in-Publication Data
Names: Lukidis, Lydia, author. | Calle, Juan, 1977–, illustrator.
Title: Deep, deep down : the secret underwater poetry of the Mariana Trench / by Lydia Lukidis; illustrated by Juan Calle.
Description: North Mankato, Minnesota : Capstone Editions, an imprint of Capstone, [2023] | Audience: Ages 8–10. | Audience: Grades 4–6. | Summary: "Deep, deep down, at the very bottom of the ocean, lies a secret world. Through lyrical narration, this spare-text STEM picture book takes readers on a journey to a place very few humans have ever been—the Mariana Trench. The imagined voyage debunks scary myths about this mysterious place with surprising and beautiful truths about life at Earth's deepest point. *Deep, Deep Down* shows a vibrant world far below and teaches readers how interconnected our lives are to every place on the planet."— Provided by publisher.
Identifiers: LCCN 2022013049 (print) | LCCN 2022013050 (ebook) | ISBN 9781684466153 (hardcover) | ISBN 9781684469451 (paperback) | ISBN 9781684466573 (pdf) | ISBN 9781684466597 (kindle edition)
Subjects: LCSH: Deep-sea ecology—Juvenile literature. | Submarine trenches—Juvenile literature. | Pelagic fish—Juvenile literature. | Biotic communities—Juvenile literature. | Mariana Trench—Juvenile literature. | LCGFT: Picture books.
Classification: LCC QH541.5.D35 L85 2023 (print) | LCC QH541.5.D35 (ebook) | DDC 577.7/9—dc23
LC record available at https://lccn.loc.gov/2022013049
LC ebook record available at https://lccn.loc.gov/2022013050

Consultant Credits
Dr. Mackenzie Gerringer, assistant professor of biology at the State University of New York at Geneseo

Designed by Kay Fraser and Jaime Willems

*Disclaimer: The illustrations in this book, while researched and accurate, are not scientifically rendered and may not be drawn to scale. All facts in the text have been researched, but our knowledge of the trench continues to evolve as we learn more about this mysterious world.

Printed and bound in China. 5593

For my daughter, the light of my life, whose curiosity and sense of wonder inspire me to no end. —L.L.

Deep,
deep
down,
at the bottom
of the Pacific Ocean
lies a secret place.

Hidden from sight,
the Mariana Trench
is the deepest underwater valley
in the world.

Do monsters lurk
at the very bottom?
Vampire squid?
Seadevil anglerfish?
Maybe giant goblin sharks,
armed with sharp,
spiky teeth?

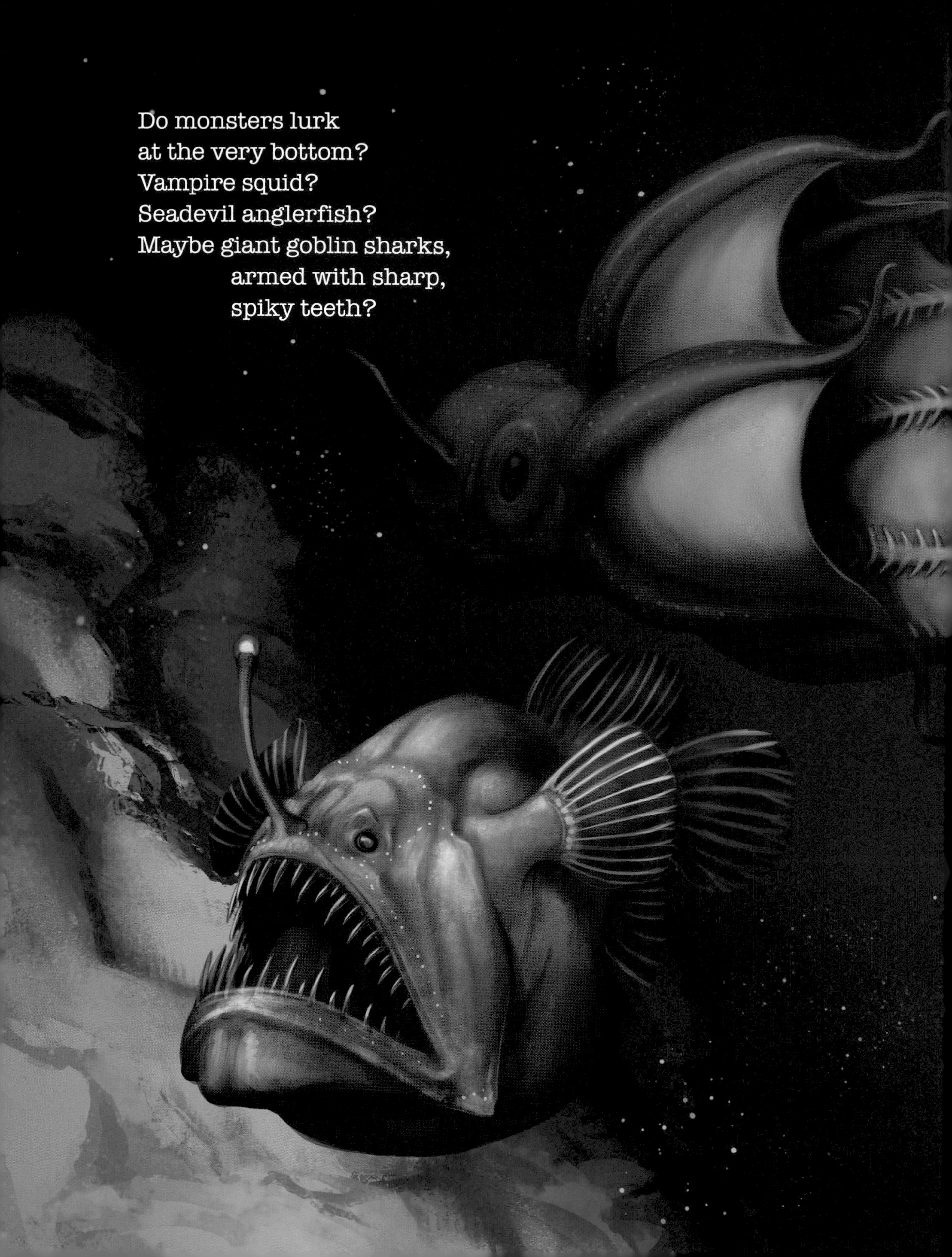

Or
perhaps the trench is
desolate
and uninhabited?

To find out,
squeeze inside the submersible and
plunge,
plunge,
plunge.

Sink down,
deeper
and deeper.
The water grows dimmer,
darker,
until the rays of sunlight
completely
disappear.

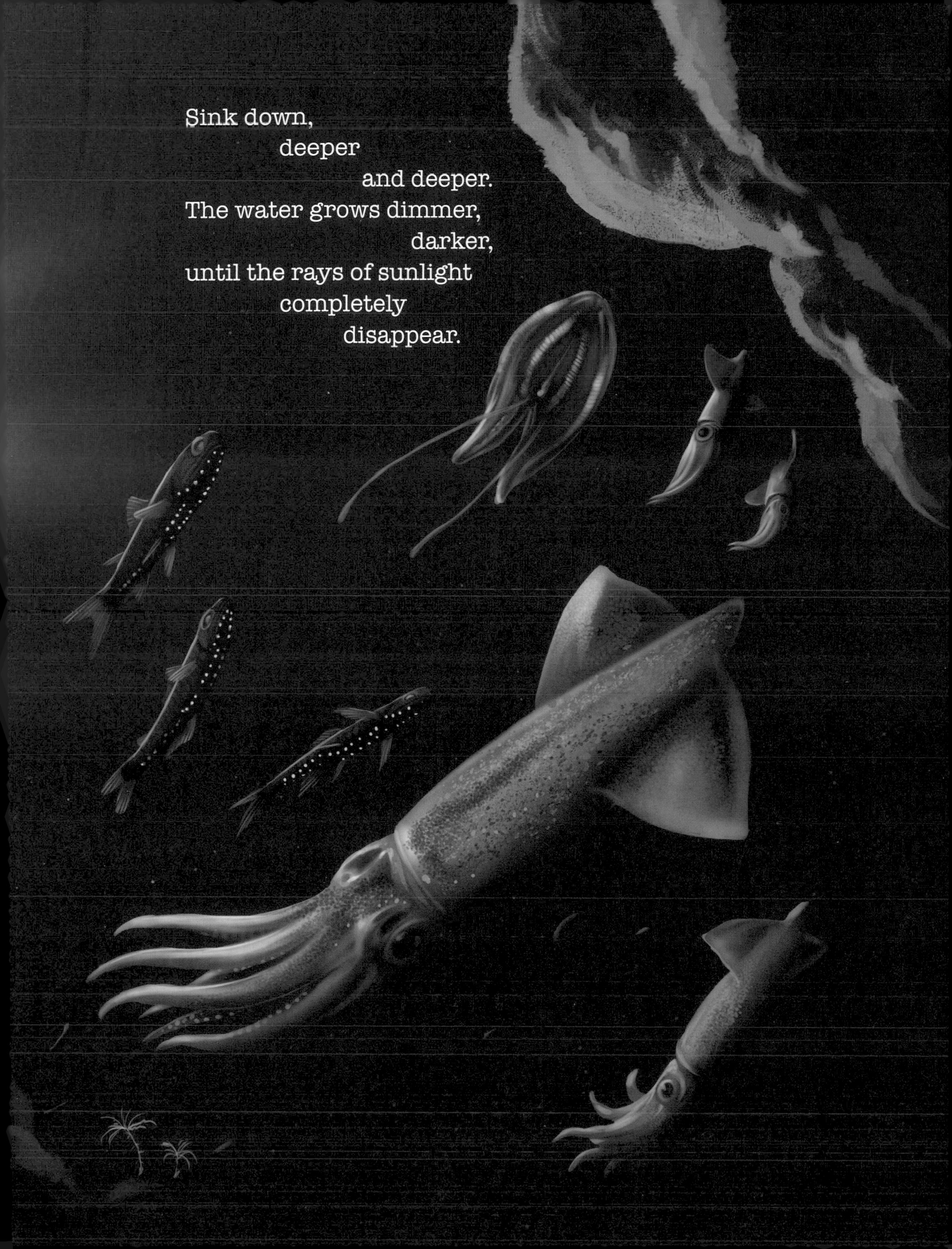

The trench,
bathed in darkness,
is a world of extremes.

Food is scarce,
and a bone-chilling cold
blasts through the water.
Earthquakes shake the ocean floor,
and the water pressure,
like a thick, heavy blanket with a thousand hands,
presses down,
down,
down.

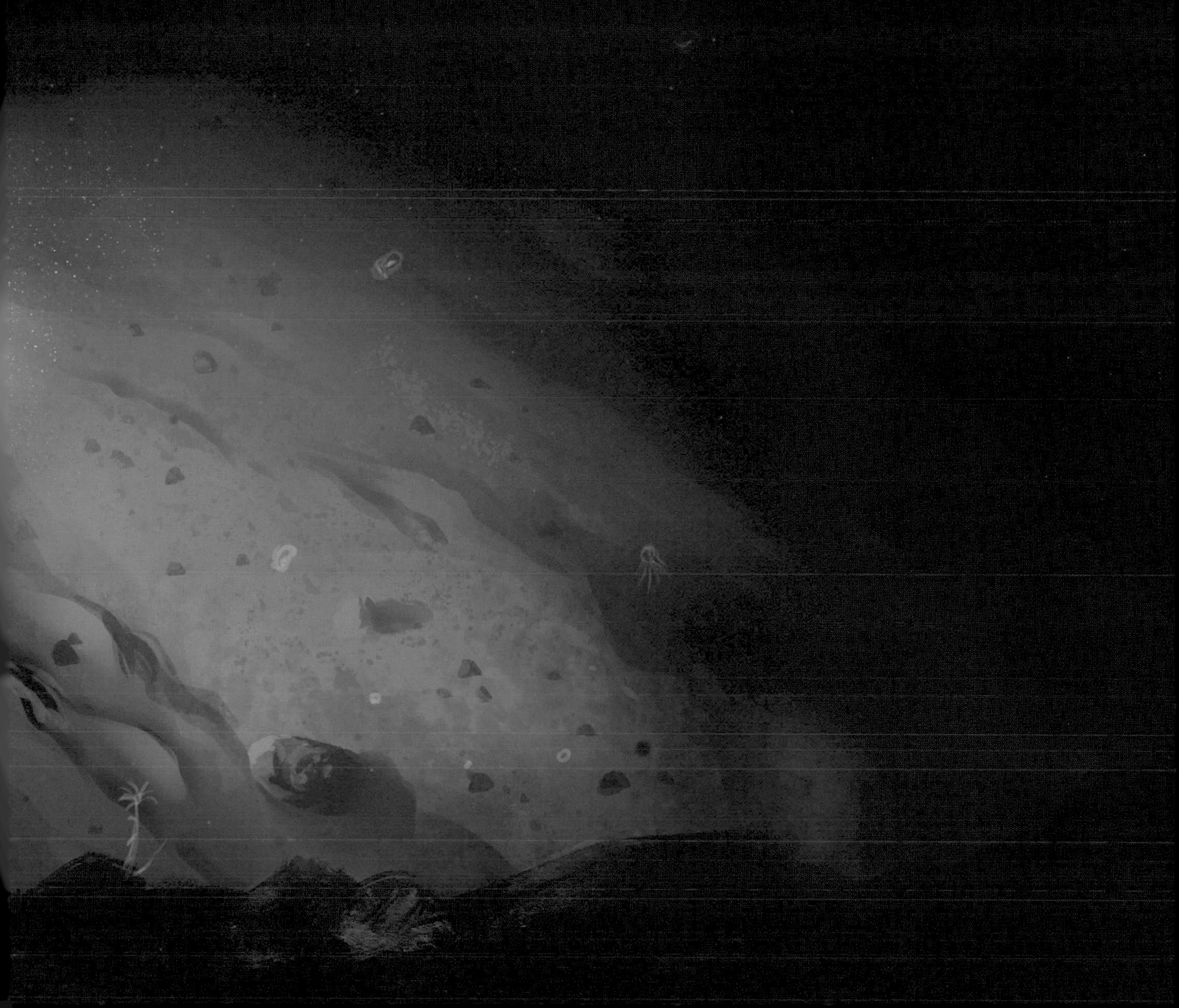

Peek out the window . . .
you are not alone.
SWISH!
Something shimmers.
Not a monster,
but a fish.
A rattail
drifts through the darkness
in search of food.

Depth: 21,000 feet (6,401 meters)
Creature: rattail, 31 inches (79 centimeters) long

Rattails have rich, fatty livers that help them survive when they can't find enough food. Similar species can survive a whopping 200 days without eating. Rattails also thrive in the dark. They can sniff out their next meal from far away with a whisker-like organ that hangs on their chins.

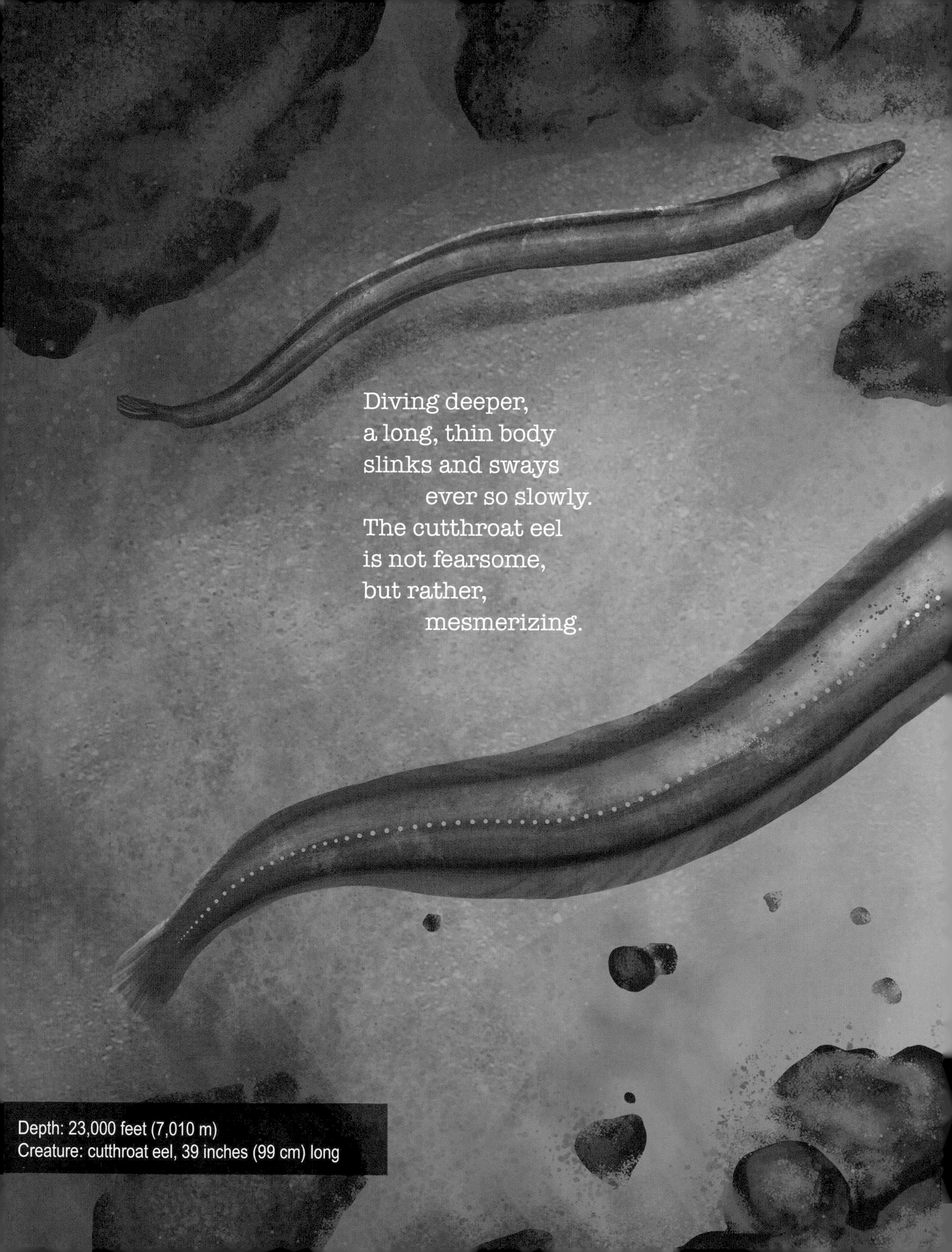

Diving deeper,
a long, thin body
slinks and sways
ever so slowly.
The cutthroat eel
is not fearsome,
but rather,
mesmerizing.

Depth: 23,000 feet (7,010 m)
Creature: cutthroat eel, 39 inches (99 cm) long

Cutthroat eels are expert swimmers. They glide forward and backward with ease and can whip around with lightning speed. Their long bodies are especially useful. Most fish quickly wag their tails or flap their fins to swim. This takes lots of energy. But cutthroat eels move their bodies ever so slowly. They don't need as much energy and can survive with little food.

A cluster of delicate branches
cartwheels by,
twirling and whirling
like an underwater acrobat.
Crinoids look like
tiny trees,
but they're wondrous creatures.
They walk
crawl
tumble
on feathery arms.

Depth: 25,000 feet (7,620 m)
Creature: crinoid, 14 inches (36 cm) long

Crinoids don't have to chase their meals. A sticky mucus on their arms traps small particles from the seawater flowing past them. Then they use their feathery arms to slide the food into their mouths. Most crinoids grow about five arms during their lifetime. But some species can grow up to 200!

Deeper still,
something glides closer.
A curious eye
presses against the window.

Depth: 27,000 feet (8,000 m)
Creature: snailfish, 7 inches (18 cm) long

A snailfish,
its thin, translucent skin stretched
over a jellylike body,
waves its delicate tail
in slow motion
as it dances, ghost-like,
to the rhythms of the ocean.

Snailfish aren't bothered by the heavy underwater pressure that pushes on deep-sea animals from all directions. They can swim deeper than any other fish in the world. That's because their bodies contain TMAO. This special substance protects the fish from high pressure, making sure their bodies aren't crushed.

Farther down,
a creature,
surprisingly small,
floats through the water.
Soon, there are dozens of amphipods,
shrimp-like,
curled tight.
Seven pairs of legs sprout
from their bodies
for walking and swimming.
Long, hairy antennae jut from their heads,
each built for smelling,
tasting,
exploring.

Depth: 31,000 feet (9,449 m)
Creature: amphipod, usually up to 1 inch (3 cm) long; in the upper parts of the trench, supergiant amphipods can reach up to 11.8 inches (30 cm)

Amphipods survive by chowing down on "marine snow"—tiny particles of algae, bacteria, and dead plants that sink down to the trench. Sometimes whales or other sea animals that live above the trench die, and their bodies float down. Amphipods can feast on these for days.

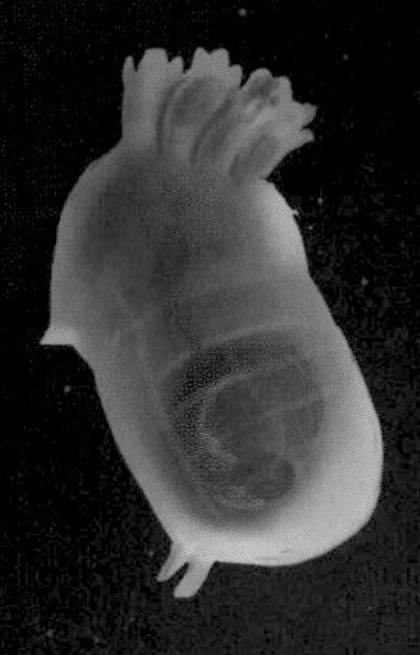

Now, sink
deep,
deep
down,
closer to the
bottom.

The Challenger Deep, the deepest part of the Mariana Trench
Depth: 35,843 feet (10,925 m)

This is the very
deepest
spot on Earth.

Look out the window . . .

. . . and witness a world of surprises.

Life thrives in the trench,
but there are no monsters in sight.
Its creatures are
small,
squishy,
and truly extraordinary.

Flashes of white twinkle
in the distance.
A soft body
sways and ripples
in an aquatic ballet.
The sea cucumber,
without a single bone in its body,
can endure the trench's crushing pressure.

Creature: sea cucumber, 3 inches (8 cm) long

Sea cucumbers have no eyes, no head, no heart, and no lungs. They hang low on the ocean floor, gobbling up mud and sand, taking in the vitamins and pooping out the rest. Deep sea cucumbers are also sensitive to temperature changes. Their bodies have adapted to the icy cold. They would die if the water became warmer.

Glide forward,
past rows and rows
of xenophyophores,
clustered like cabbages.
Their protective shells
are like little houses,
each one a home
to its tiny neighbors.

Creature: xenophyophorea, 4 inches (10 cm) long

Xenophyophores are neither plants nor animals, though they're alive. They're single-celled organisms. But xenophyophores are gigantic, with some as big as soccer balls. Their shells are made up of bits of dirt, dead animals, rocks, and minerals stuck together with a cement-like glue that contains their poop.

The Mariana Trench,
a world of wonder and
surprise,
teems with life.
Its diverse creatures flow
and dance with the currents,
gracefully,
like underwater poetry.

Depth: 3,000 feet (914 m)

Grab one last glimpse
as the submersible slowly inches
up,
up,
up,
bidding the trench farewell.

Rays of sunlight
glimmer through the waves.

And then . . .

SPLASH!

The submersible surfaces,
leaving the marvels
of the Mariana Trench
far below.

But the trench's icy waters
still hold many secrets,
hiding,
waiting,
yet to be discovered.

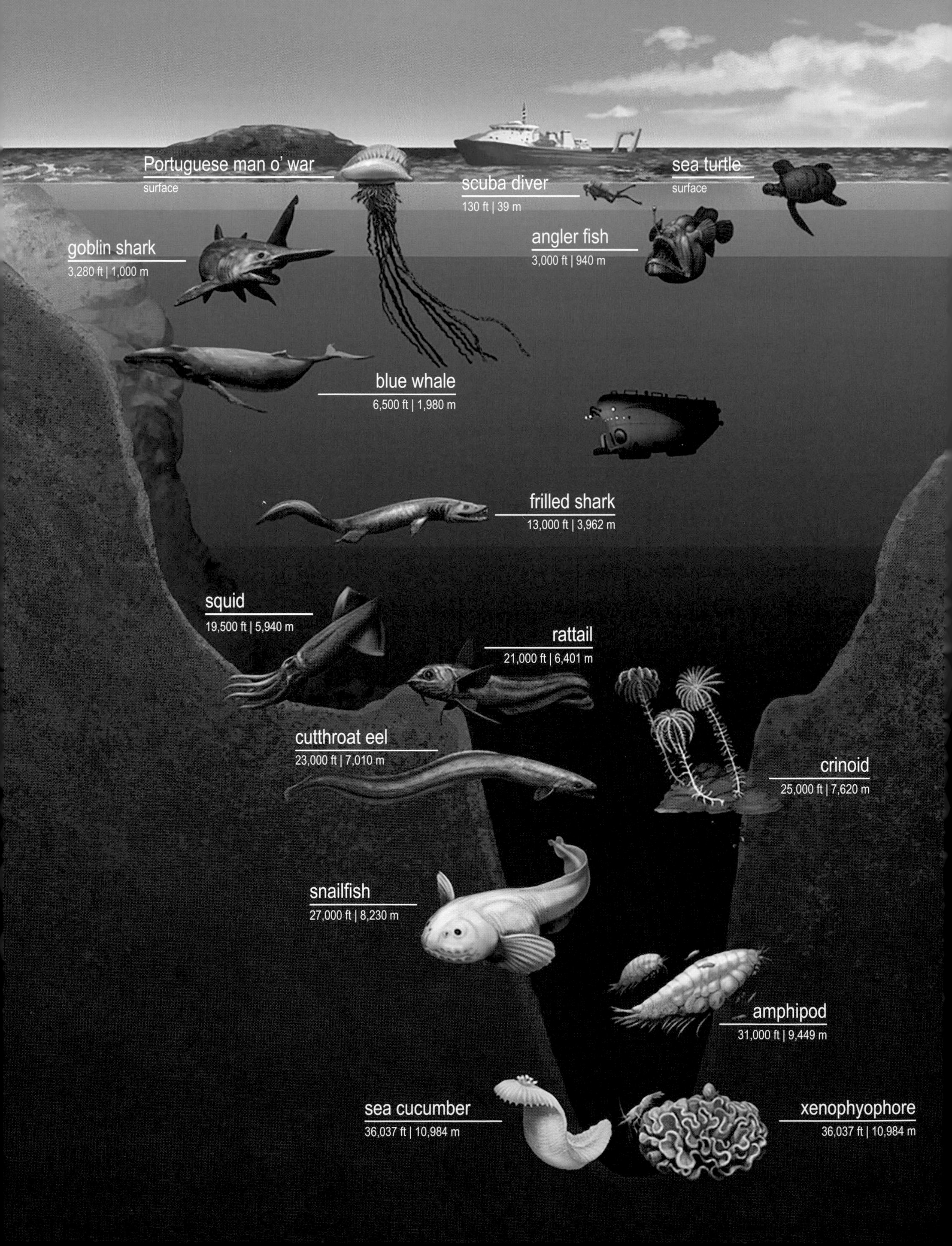

Portuguese man o' war
surface
scuba diver
130 ft | 39 m
sea turtle
surface
goblin shark
3,280 ft | 1,000 m
angler fish
3,000 ft | 940 m
blue whale
6,500 ft | 1,980 m
frilled shark
13,000 ft | 3,962 m
squid
19,500 ft | 5,940 m
rattail
21,000 ft | 6,401 m
cutthroat eel
23,000 ft | 7,010 m
crinoid
25,000 ft | 7,620 m
snailfish
27,000 ft | 8,230 m
amphipod
31,000 ft | 9,449 m
sea cucumber
36,037 ft | 10,984 m
xenophyophore
36,037 ft | 10,984 m

Did You Know?

How deep is it?

The Mariana Trench lies hidden at the bottom of the western Pacific Ocean. At the deepest point (called the Challenger Deep), it plummets to 35,843 feet (10,925 meters) below sea level. How deep is that? If you placed Mount Everest, one of the tallest mountains on Earth, at the bottom of the trench, the peak would still be more than 7,000 feet (2,143 meters) below sea level!

What's the water pressure like?

The water in the ocean presses against everything in it. This pressure increases the deeper you go. The pressure at the bottom of the Mariana Trench is 1,100 times higher than at sea level. Wonder what that feels like? Imagine an adult elephant standing on your toe. Underwater, that pressure pushes against your body in all directions. OUCH!

Did the Mariana Trench exist when Earth was created?

Nope! Scientists believe it formed about 50 million years ago. But how? The earth, including the land beneath the oceans, is divided into different plates—large sheets of rock that are part of Earth's crust. Imagine our whole planet like a jigsaw puzzle, with pieces that can move around. Sometimes, when two plates slam into each other, one of them forces the other downward. That's how the Mariana Trench formed.

Why isn't there much food in the trench?

The Mariana Trench is so deep that no sunlight reaches it. The food created at the top of the ocean has to sink all the way to the bottom. Other sea animals that live above the trench gobble most of it up before it can reach the trench. Only about one percent of the food produced at the surface of the ocean makes it into the trench.

How many people have visited the trench?

In 1960, United States Navy Lieutenant Don Walsh and Swiss engineer Jacques Piccard became the first humans to make the journey to the bottom of the Mariana Trench. Before their dive, their submersible was tested more than 60 times to make sure it could survive the bone-crushing pressure. As of March 2022, about two dozen people have journeyed to the depths of the Mariana Trench. That's about as many as have visited the moon! But scientists are currently heading up projects to explore the trench further.

Why Does the Mariana Trench Matter?

The Mariana Trench is a natural wonder and one of the most unique habitats in the world. Discovering the trench and the creatures that live there has changed the way we see science and life itself. That's why, in 2009, the United States created the Marianas Trench Marine National Monument. It preserves and protects 95,216 square miles (246,608 square kilometers) of underwater lands and waters. Read on to understand more about *why* the Mariana Trench is so important.

Human curiosity

We like to explore our world. We want to go to the moon, see the deepest parts of the ocean, and discover what lies beyond our current borders. We also want to understand the limits of life. Studying the trench helps us learn how deep animals can live, the most extreme temperatures animals and microbes can survive in, and the strangest adaptations on our planet.

Exploring our world and beyond

The Marianas Trench Marine National Monument holds secrets that contribute to science and help us understand our world. And when we examine how life thrives in hostile conditions, like the trench, we begin to wonder if life can also exist on other planets. Many researchers studying the trench also work for The National Aeronautics and Space Administration (NASA) and are looking for these answers.

Understanding earthquakes and volcanoes

Did you know that all of the world's biggest earthquakes occur near trenches? These violent movements of the ocean floor can also cause tsunamis—gigantic ocean waves created by undersea earthquakes—landslides, and volcanic eruptions that shape our world. For example, some western Pacific trenches have neighboring island chains, like Japan, the Philippines, and Indonesia, that were formed by volcanoes. Understanding how the geologic forces in the trenches work will help scientists better inform people about huge earthquakes before they happen. Studying volcanoes can also help us understand how life began billions of years ago.

Everything is connected

The entire ocean, including the Mariana Trench, is an ecosystem that works together. And no matter how isolated the trench may seem, humans do affect it. In 2019, an explorer discovered a plastic bag floating in the Mariana Trench. Researchers also found plastic and other chemicals in the stomachs of some sea animals in the trench. Ocean pollution affects the entire ecosystem and throws it off-balance.

Biodiversity

The Marianas Trench Marine National Monument is jam-packed with islands, mud volcanoes, rare coral reefs, underwater chimneys, acids, gases, and boiling water. These unique features give rise to diverse life forms, including unusual species and others yet to be discovered. Biodiversity is important for life on Earth because plants, animals, and humans depend on each other for survival. Losing just one species can harm many others.

A Note from the Author

When I first heard about the Mariana Trench years ago, I wondered what kind of creatures lurked at the very bottom. Motivated by curiosity, I began my research. I stumbled upon several websites that claimed fearsome animals roamed the deepest place on Earth.

A sea of monsters! That's exactly what I'd imagined. But after speaking with several experts, I discovered much of the online information about the Mariana Trench is false. The trench is not inhabited by "monsters" or prehistoric-looking creatures, like some claimed. There aren't even any sharks in the trench—they can't survive deeper than 13,000 feet (3,962 meters).

Ultimately, I discovered that the creatures of the trench are small, soft, and gooey, with mostly white or translucent skin. And despite the trench's hostile conditions, it's full of diverse life. I found footage taken by researchers who dropped traps with cameras to the bottom of the trench. I watched the videos over and over, completely fascinated by these strange animals and how they manage to survive in such a harsh environment. I was equally mesmerized by their slow, graceful movements, like underwater poetry. That's when I realized: the Mariana Trench itself is a poem, and it inspired me to write this book.

Acknowledgements

I'm eternally grateful to the experts who helped make this book a reality. I would like to thank Dr. Mackenzie Gerringer for her expertise, knowledge, and willingness to answer my questions—and there were many! I'm also grateful to Dr. Patricia Fryer, Dr. Christopher Mah, Dr. Jeffrey Drazen, Professor Alan Jamieson, and Lieutenant Don Walsh, USN for their valuable contributions and for being pioneers in their respective fields.

Glossary

adaptation (a-dap-TAY-shuhn)—a change a living thing goes through to better fit in with its environment

aquatic (uh-KWAH-tik)—living or growing in water

barren (BA-ruhn)—not producing; unfruitful

biodiversity (BYE-oh-dih-VURS-uh-tee)—variety of life in genetics, species, and ecosystems

cell (SEL)—the smallest unit of a living thing; most cells are so small they can't be seen without a microscope

current (KUHR-uhnt)—the movement of water in a river or ocean

diverse (dih-VURS)—different from each other

ecosystem (EE-koh-sis-tuhm)—a system of living and nonliving things in an environment

hostile (HOSS-tuhl)—unfriendly or angry

microbe (MYE-krobe)—a tiny living thing that is too small to be seen without a microscope

plate (PLAYT)—a large sheet of rock that is a piece of Earth's crust

scarce (SKAIRS)—hard to find

submersible (suhb-MURS-uh-buhl)—a small vessel used under water, usually for research

translucent (trans-LOO-suhnt)—partially see-through; allowing some rays of light to pass through

trench (TRENCH)—a long, narrow steep-sided hole in the ocean floor

water pressure (WAT-ur PRESH-ur)—the force that water exerts; pressure increases with the depth of the ocean

photo credit: Magenta Photo

About the Author

Lydia Lukidis is the author of more than 48 trade and educational books, as well as 30 e-books. Her STEM title, *The Broken Bees' Nest* (Kane Press, 2019), was nominated for a Cybils Award. Lydia is passionate about fostering love for children's literacy. In addition to offering writing workshops and author visits in elementary schools, she's very involved in the kidlit community and volunteers as a judge on Rate Your Story. For more information, please visit www.lydialukidis.com.

photo credit: Santiago Calle

About the Illustrator

Juan Calle is a former biologist turned science illustrator who trained at California State University, Monterey Bay's science illustration program. Early in his career as an illustrator, Juan created field guides of plants and animals in his home country, Colombia. He now owns and works in his own art studio, LIBERUM DONUM, in Bogota, Colombia, creating concept art, storyboarding, and working on his other passion—comic books.